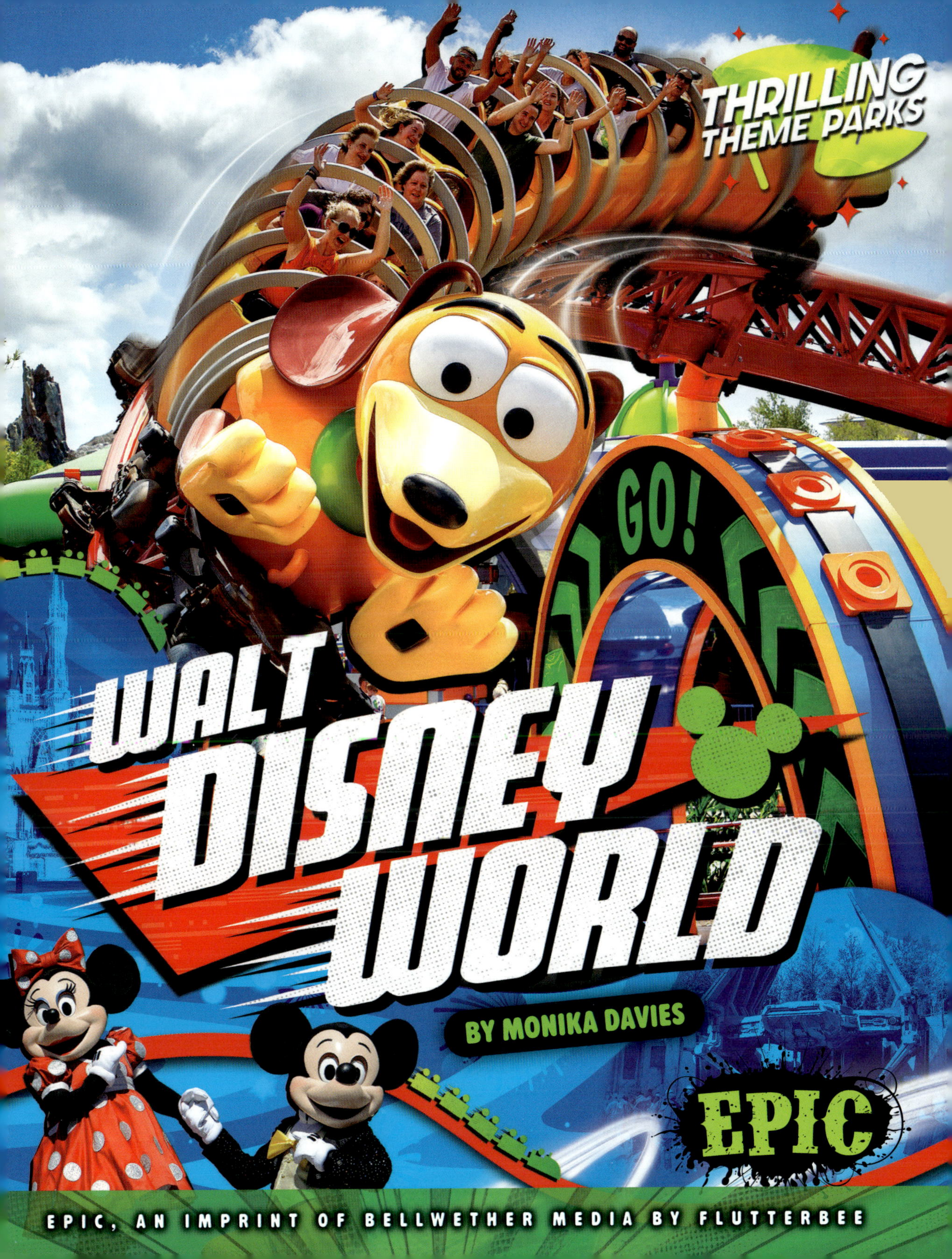
THRILLING THEME PARKS
GO!
WALT DISNEY WORLD
BY MONIKA DAVIES
EPIC
EPIC, AN IMPRINT OF BELLWETHER MEDIA BY FLUTTERBEE

EPIC

EPIC BOOKS are no ordinary books. They burst with intense action, high-speed heroics, and shadows of the unknown. Are you ready for an Epic adventure?

This edition first published in 2027 by Bellwether Media, Inc.

For information regarding permission, write to Bellwether Media, Inc., Attention: Permissions Department, 3500 American Blvd W, Suite 150, Bloomington, MN 55431.

Library of Congress Cataloging-in-Publication Data

Names: Davies, Monika author
Title: Walt Disney World / by Monika Davies.
Description: Minneapolis, Minnesota : Bellwether Media, Inc, 2027. | Series: Thrilling theme parks | Includes bibliographical references and index. | Audience: Ages 8-12 | Audience: Grades 4-6 | Summary: "Engaging images accompany information about Disney World. The combination of high-interest subject matter and light text is intended for students in grades 2 through 7"--Provided by publisher.
Identifiers: LCCN 2026010734 (print) | LCCN 2026010735 (ebook) | ISBN 9798898801014 library binding | ISBN 9798898802257 ebook
Subjects: LCSH: Walt Disney World (Fla.)--History | Amusement parks--Florida | Disney, Walt, 1901-1966
Classification: LCC GV1853.3.F62 D38 2027 (print) | LCC GV1853.3.F62 (ebook) | DDC 791.068759/24--dc23/eng/20260313
LC record available at https://lccn.loc.gov/2026010734
LC ebook record available at https://lccn.loc.gov/2026010735

Editor: Elizabeth Neuenfeldt Designer: Gabriel Hilger

Printed in the United States of America, North Mankato, MN.

TABLE OF CONTENTS

THE MOST MAGICAL PLACE ON EARTH

A family walks down Main Street, U.S.A. Cheerful music adds a pep to their steps. Mickey Mouse waves at them.

Ahead, a castle **shimmers**. The family gazes in **awe**. It looks just like the movies!

MICKEY MOUSE

PICTURE PERFECT

Special paint is used for Walt Disney World's Cinderella Castle! The paint can stay in the sun for a long time and not lose its color.

There are six Disney **resorts**. Walt Disney World is the largest. It is near Orlando, Florida.

HOLLYWOOD STUDIOS

ENDLESS WONDER

In 2024, there were 87 rides and shows at Walt Disney World!

WALT DISNEY WORLD MAP

Walt Disney World has four **theme parks**. These include the Magic Kingdom, EPCOT, Hollywood Studios, and Animal Kingdom.

THE MAKING OF WALT DISNEY WORLD

BORN 1901

ROLE
Founder

ACCOMPLISHMENTS
Made cartoon films and built Disneyland

WALT DISNEY

Walt Disney was a person. He first made movies. He dreamed of building a park. He wanted it to be a magical and **immersive** experience.

Walt opened Disneyland. It is in California. The rides are based on Disney films.

Walt wanted to build a bigger park. He began to buy land in Florida.

He died in 1966. His brother Roy took over the project. He wanted to keep Walt's dream alive.

It took 18 months of **construction**. Over 9,000 people worked on the park. In 1971, Walt Disney World opened.

MAIN STREET, U.S.A., IN 1975

THE GRAND OPENING

People were excited for Walt Disney World's opening! Around 10,000 people visited the park on opening day.

DUMBO THE FLYING ELEPHANT

At first, the park only had the Magic Kingdom. Popular rides included Dumbo the Flying Elephant and the Haunted Mansion.

Walt Disney World grew. EPCOT opened in 1982. What is now Hollywood Studios opened in 1989.

Animal Kingdom opened in 1998. People can spot hippos and other live animals there!

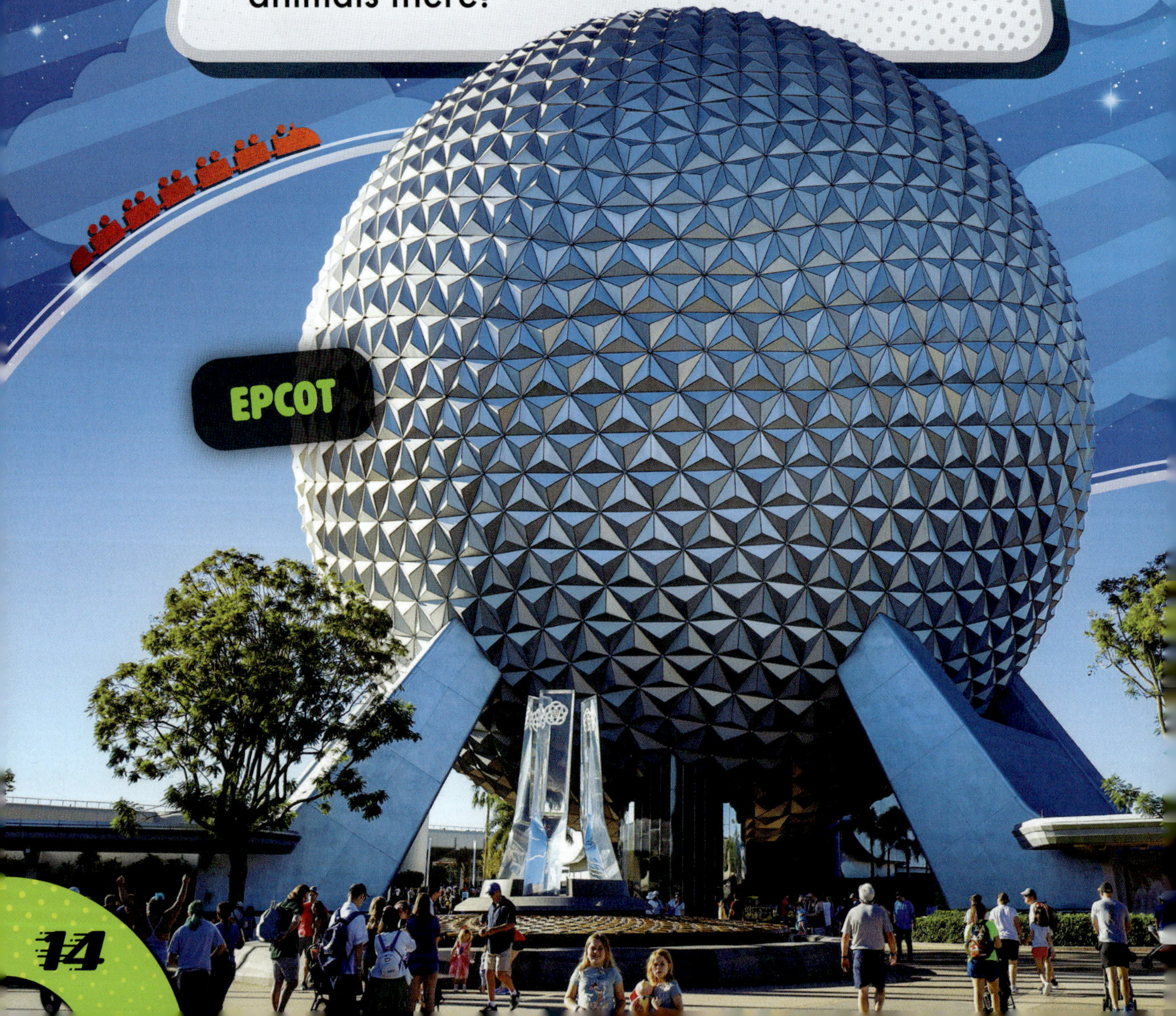

The Magic Kingdom Attendance Records

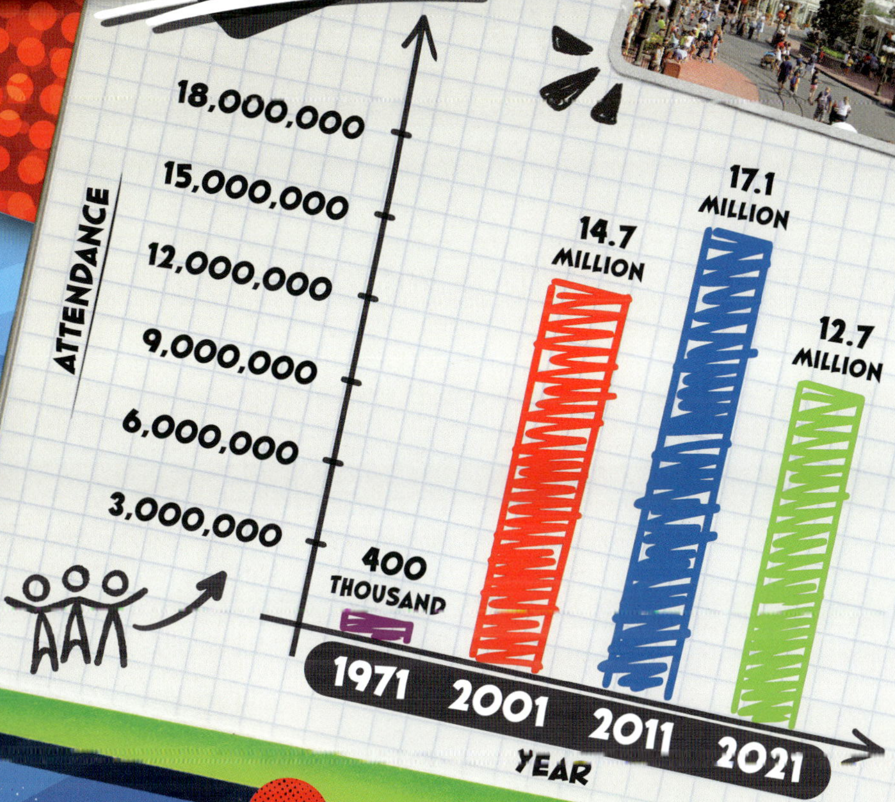

ANIMAL KINGDOM

WALT DISNEY WORLD TODAY

There is always something new at Walt Disney World. Fresh events take place. New rides open.

Monstropolis is planned to open in 2028. It is **inspired** by *Monsters, Inc.* People will explore the film's monster factory.

THE HAUNTED MANSION

WHAT IS IT?

A ride through a ghost-filled mansion

STAT

There are 160 doom buggies that riders ride in.

FUN FACT

The ride says it has 999 happy haunts.

Villains Land is in the works too. Two new **attractions** will open.

People often visit Walt Disney World **multiple** times. No one can see all of the parks in one day!

WALT DISNEY WORLD EVENTS

Walt Disney World has many fan events. Mickey's Not-So-Scary Halloween Party is in the fall. People wear costumes. They watch parades.

Disney Princess Half Marathon Weekend

DATE
February or March

LOCATIONS
EPCOT and Magic Kingdom

EVENT
People run with Disney princesses for different distances.

At the park, fans wear Mickey Mouse ears. It is a classic **souvenir** from a magical park!

Glossary

attractions—interesting things that people want to see or visit

awe—a strong feeling of wonder

construction—the process of building something

immersive—seems to surround someone so they feel completely involved in what is going on

inspired—gave someone an idea about what to do or create

multiple—more than one

resorts—places that have things to do for people who are on vacation

shimmers—shines with lights that seem to move

souvenir—something a person keeps as a reminder of a place they visited

theme parks—parks where the rides and shows are based on certain subjects

To Learn More

AT THE LIBRARY

Krensky, Stephen. *Walt Disney*. New York, N.Y.: Crabtree Publishing, 2025.

National Geographic Kids. *Disney: 300 Wonderful Facts to Celebrate the Magic of Disney*. Washington, D.C.: National Geographic, 2023.

Ventura, Marne. *Walt Disney World*. Minneapolis, Minn.: Abdo Publishing, 2020.

ON THE WEB

FACTSURFER

Factsurfer.com gives you a safe, fun way to find more information.

1. Go to www.factsurfer.com.

2. Enter "Walt Disney World" into the search box and click .

3. Select your book cover to see a list of related content.

Index

The images in this book are reproduced through the courtesy of: Craig Russell, front cover, p. 1; Eden, Janine and Jim/ Wikimedia Commons, fornt cover, p. 1; lucky-photo, front cover, p. 1; Helen Sessions/ Alamy Stock Photo, front cover, p. 1; Senior Airman Dakota C. LeGrand/ Wikimedia Commons, pp. 2-3; Featureflash Photo Agency, p. 3; Handout/ Handout/ Getty Images, pp. 4, 20; RSBPhoto1/ Alamy Stock Photo, p. 5; Joni Hanebutt/ Alamy Stock Photo, pp. 6, 16; Dennis MacDonald, p. 7; Mlang.Finn/ Wikimedia Commons, p. 8; Classic Cinema Archive/ Alamy Stock Photo, p. 8 (inset); From Original Negative/ Alamy Stock Photo, p. 9; Joe Myeress/ Alamy Stock Photo, p. 10; Florida Development Commission/ Wikimedia Commons, p. 11; D Guest Smith/ Alamy Stock Photo, p. 12; Miami Herald/ Contributor/ Getty Images, p. 13; Jedi94/ Wikimedia Commons, pp. 14, 15 (Animal Kingdom); Theme Park Tourist/ Wikimedia Commons, p. 15 (attendance); M2 Photography/ Alamy Stock Photo, p. 17; DearCatastropheWaitress/ Wikimedia Commons, p. 17 (sign); Gary Hershorn/ Contributor/ Getty Images, pp. 18-19; Gerardo Mora/ Contributor/ Getty Images, p. 21.